Rosa Parks

A Biography Funbook™

By Carole Marsh

A Word From the Author...

Rosa Parks was a civil rights activist. She is best known for her bravery when she refused to give up her seat on a public bus to a White man. Little did she know what kind of massive movement that one small refusal would start!

-Carole Marsh

About the Author...

Carole marsh is the creator of the  and author of many books on History, Geography, and Biography. She is also the creator of The 50 State Experience Series, which includes books, workbooks, software, stickers, maps, and other products for all 50 States and Canada. You can write to her at gallopade@gallopade.com.

Rosa Parks

mother of the Civil Rights movement

Rosa Louise McCauley was born in Tuskegee, Alabama on February 4, 1913. While she was still young, she moved with her mother and brother to her grandparents' farm in Pine Level, Alabama.

Unscramble the words in the sentence below to learn more about Rosa's family.

Rosa's ________ was a ________ and
     OETHMR   ECHATER

her _______ was a carpenter.
    ERFAHT

Rosa married Raymond Parks in 1932. Raymond was a barber. Both he and Rosa became active in different civil rights causes, especially Black voter rights. Rosa worked with the Youth Council of the National Association for the Advancement of Colored People (NAACP) as a volunteer.

Connect the dots to find one of the tools Raymond Parks used as a barber.

1. 2. 3. 4. 5. 6. 7. 8. 9. 10. 11. 12. 13. 14. 15. 16. 17. 18. 19. 20. 21.

Rosa's help in the NAACP led her to be elected as their montgomery secretary in 1943.

Through her volunteer work with the NAACP, Rosa helped in the efforts to overcome racial segregation in education and also in public places. This was a difficult task and progress was slow.

Color the money.

To learn what some of Rosa's paying jobs were, solve the code below.

A	B	C	D	E	F	G	H	I	J	K	L	M

N	O	P	Q	R	S	T	U	V	W	X	Y	Z

and

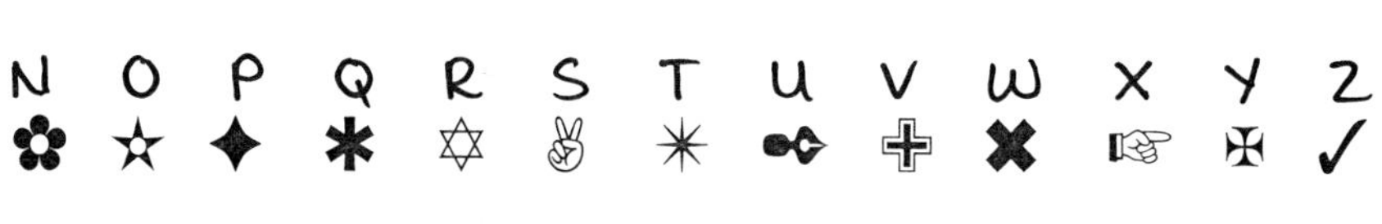

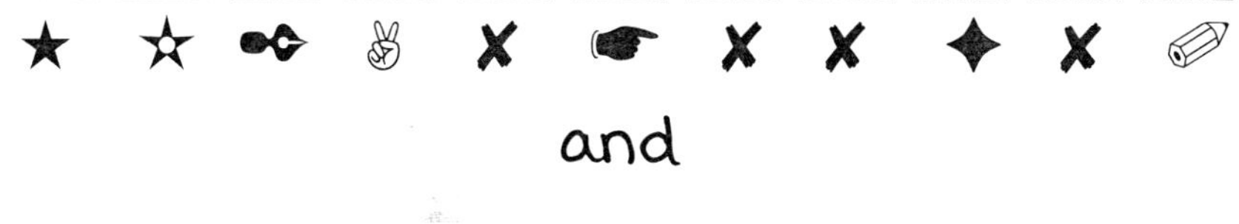

Like many others, Rosa depended on the city bus to get to work. In Montgomery, the first ten seats of every bus were for White passengers. African American passengers could not sit in these seats even if there were no White passengers on the bus.

Color the city bus.

The separation of Black and White people on the city buses in Montgomery was an example of _________________. Place a check beside the correct answer.

____segregation

____equality

____fairness

If White sections were full, African American people were required to give up their seats to White people.

On December 1, 1955, Rosa boarded a bus after a long day at work. She sat in the back section of the bus, along with three other African American passengers. When all of the seats for White people were filled, Rosa and the other African American passengers were told to give up their seats as more White passengers got on the bus. Rosa refused.

At first, the other African American passengers refused to give up their seats also. When the driver threatened that he would call the police, the three gave up their seats. Rosa still refused and was arrested. She was taken to jail and fined $14.

In what Alabama city did this event take place? Circle your answer.

Tallahassee

Richmond

Montgomery

Rosa's arrest interested E.D. Nixon, an African American community leader. He asked her if he could use her case to try to bring an end to segregation on the buses in montgomery. Rosa bravely said, "Yes!"

Rosa's mother and husband feared for Rosa's safety if she agreed to Nixon's idea.

Find the words in the Word Find below.

ROSA   RIGHTS   BUS

R	L	A	W	R
T	O	B	I	A
T	S	S	N	C
O	C	W	A	B
C	D	X	J	R
Y	X	E	M	Q
O	K	W	S	J
B	T	S	E	R

Color the pencil.

E.D. Nixon and others got together to plan the strategy for a bus boycott. Many community organizations and churches helped spread the word. Flyers were also printed, telling of Rosa's arrest and urging people not to ride the buses on December 5.

BOYCOTT		ARREST		LAW
X	E	S	T	P
M	B	U	R	K
H	V	E	I	Y
U	S	I	G	K
I	G	T	H	A
A	K	S	T	O
B	P	L	S	M
R	A	T	H	K

Rosa lost her job as a seamstress as a result of the bus boycott. She and her husband continued to be harassed in Montgomery. In 1957, they decided to move to Detroit, Michigan to find work. In Detroit, they had a hard time finding jobs and were homeless for a while.

Even through these rough times, Rosa remained active in the NAACP.

Put the following events in order.

_____ Rosa married Raymond Parks.

_____ Rosa was arrested and fined.

_____ Rosa moved to Detroit.

_____ Rosa refused to give up her bus seat.

In 1965, Rosa finally found steady work in the office of U.S. Congressman John Conyers, Jr., a civil rights leader in Congress.

Rosa continued to work for John Conyers, Jr. for over 20 years. Her husband, Raymond, died in 1977, two years before Rosa won the Springarn medal for her work in civil rights. She continued to receive numerous awards and honors in recognition of her work.

In 1987, Rosa founded the Rosa and Raymond Parks Institute for Self-Development to provide career training for young people.

Color the picture of Rosa and her awards.

Rosa never had any children.

In 1992, Rosa published her autobiography Rosa Parks: My Story. In 1995, she took part in the million man march in Washington, D.C. where she gave an inspirational speech. Rosa died in her home on October 25, 2005.

In July of 1999, President Bill Clinton awarded Rosa the nation's highest civilian honor. To learn the name of this award, cross off every other letter below, starting with the letter B.

B C H O T N R G E R I E Z S P S Y I B
O V N M A K L O G X O E L Q D N M
R E A D I A G L U H P O B N E O W R

_ _ _ _ _ _ _ _ _ _ _ _ _ _ _ _

_ _ _ _ _ _   _ _ _ _ _ _

of   _ _ _ _ _ _ _

GLOSSARY

autobiography: a story of one's own life, written by oneself

boycott: to join with others and refuse to buy, sell, or use something

civilian: a person who is not a member of the armed forces

harassed: to worry or trouble; to trouble by attacking again and again

segregation: forcing people of different racial groups to live apart from each other, go to separate schools, and use separate public facilities

AMAZING ROSA!

Help Rosa find her way to work from the bus stop.

POP QUIZ!

1. Rosa's mother was a:
   - ○ A. teacher
   - ○ B. nurse
   - ○ C. minister

2. Rosa volunteered for the:
   - ○ A. Sierra Club
   - ○ B. NAACP
   - ○ C. Humane Society

3. Rosa's arrest started the_______bus boycott.
   - ○ A. Philadelphia
   - ○ B. Atlanta
   - ○ C. Montgomery

4. Rosa and her husband moved from Alabama to:
   - ○ A. Indiana
   - ○ B. Florida
   - ○ C. Michigan

5. Rosa was awarded the Congressional Gold Medal of Honor in:
   - ○ A. 1950
   - ○ B. 1972
   - ○ C. 1999

-mendous Trivia!

Whee! I feel like I'm hang-gliding!

After Rosa's death, her body was viewed at the U.S. Capital Rotunda.

She was the first woman to be laid in state there.

Do squirrels eat ladybugs?!

Rosa had a previous encounter with the bus driver.

The Montgomery bus boycott was only supposed to last a day.

How many did you get right?

Answer Key
Page 1: Mother, teacher, father; Page 3: housekeeper; Page 4: segregation; Page 5: Montgomery; Page 8: 1, 3, 4, 2; Page 10: Congressional gold medal honor; Pop Quiz: teacher, NAACP, Montgomery, Michigan, 1999.